WORLD WAR II
LEADERS AND
GENERALS

BY JOHN HAMILTON

VISIT US AT
WWW.ABDOPUBLISHING.COM

Published by ABDO Publishing Company, 8000 West 78th Street, Suite 310, Edina, MN 55439.

Printed in the United States of America, North Mankato, Minnesota.
082011
092011

♻ PRINTED ON RECYCLED PAPER

Editor: Sue Hamilton
Graphic Design: John Hamilton
Cover Design: Neil Klinepier
Cover Photo: National Archives and Records Administration (NARA)
Interior Photos and Illustrations: Alamy-pgs 28 (background & bottom photos) & 29 (background, top & bottom); AP-pgs 14-15, 18-20, 22, 26 & 27 (top); Corbis-pgs 8-13 & 25; Digital Stock-pgs 1 & 23; Getty Images-pgs 16, 17, 21 & 26-27 (background), Granger Collection-pgs 4-7, 27 (middle & bottom) & 28 (top); Library of Congress-pg 7; NARA-pg 24.

ABDO Booklinks
To learn more about World War II, visit ABDO Publishing Company online. Web sites about World War II are featured on our Book Links pages. These links are routinely monitored and updated to provide the most current information available. Web site: www.abdopublishing.com

Library of Congress Cataloging-in-Publication Data

Hamilton, John, 1959-
  World War II : leaders and generals / John Hamilton.
    p. cm. -- (World War II)
  Includes index.
  ISBN 978-1-61783-061-7
  1. World War, 1939-1945--Biography--Juvenile literature. 2. Heads of state--Biography--Juvenile literature. I. Title.
  D736.H34 2012
  940.53092'2--dc23
                                2011020131

CONTENTS

The victory meeting of American generals in 1945.

AXIS AND ALLIES

Winston Churchill

Franklin Roosevelt

Joseph Stalin

The political and military leaders of World War II are some of the most famous people in history. Some of them were murderous dictators responsible for the deaths of millions of people. Others were heroic and visionary. Some had the burden of leadership thrust upon them, and did their best during difficult times. The actions and policies of these people led their citizens through the most destructive period of time the world has ever seen.

World War II officially began in September 1939, when Germany invaded neighboring Poland. But many historians see World War II as an extension of an earlier war, World War I (1914-1918), the "war to end all wars." Many of the leaders and generals of World War II were greatly influenced by the misery and destruction caused by World War I. They were also influenced by the economic catastrophe of the Great Depression of the 1930s.

Italy's Benito Mussolini (hand raised) and Germany's Adolf Hitler formed an alliance with Japan's Emperor Hirohito to become the Axis powers.

Many leaders, called isolationists, vowed that their countries would never again fight in such a big war. Other leaders, especially Adolf Hitler from Germany, sought revenge against old enemies. Hitler, together with Emperor Hirohito from Japan and Benito Mussolini from Italy, formed an alliance called the Axis powers. They wanted to expand their nations' control, even if it meant more war.

Many nations fought against the Axis. They were known as the Allies. The most important leaders among them were President Franklin Roosevelt of the United States, Prime Minister Winston Churchill of the United Kingdom, and Joseph Stalin of the Soviet Union. These men were called the "Big Three."

Many things decided the winners and losers of World War II, including resources, weapons, and even luck. But the most important advantage of the Allies was the guidance of their leaders.

FRANKLIN DELANO ROOSEVELT

1882–1945

Franklin Delano Roosevelt (1882-1945) was the 32nd president of the United States from 1933 to 1945. He was a strong leader who guided America through some of its worst times, including the Great Depression and most of World War II.

Despite being confined to a wheelchair (he contracted polio in 1921), Roosevelt's optimistic personality and his use of government programs to help the economy restored the nation's confidence.

In the late 1930s, as Germany and Japan became more aggressive, Roosevelt kept the United States officially neutral. But when Japan attacked the American naval base at Pearl Harbor, Hawaii, on December 7, 1941, Roosevelt said it was "a date which will live in infamy." The United States declared war on the Axis countries shortly afterwards.

During the war, Roosevelt worked tirelessly with the United Kingdom's Winston Churchill and the Soviet Union's Joseph Stalin. Together they were called the "Big Three." Roosevelt let his generals make important military decisions, but his policies improved the industrial might of the United States, which greatly helped the Allied war effort.

Franklin Roosevelt died on April 12, 1945, just a few months before the end of the war. He was succeeded by President Harry S. Truman (1884-1972).

Harry S. Truman became president of the United States after the death of Franklin Roosevelt.

HARRY S. TRUMAN 1884–1972

WINSTON
CHURCHILL

1874– 1965

Sir Winston Churchill (1874-1965) was prime minister of the United Kingdom during most of World War II, from 1940-1945 (and again from 1951-1955). He was a brilliant speechmaker and shrewd politician. During the war, he was often seen in public flashing his famous "V for victory" hand gesture.

In the 1930s, Churchill recognized the threat of Nazi Germany. He warned that Prime Minister Neville Chamberlain's policies of appeasement, of giving in to German demands, would not stop Adolf Hitler's ambition to conquer Europe. In September 1939, Germany invaded Poland, followed by Denmark and Norway in April 1940. Chamberlain resigned as prime minister and was replaced by Churchill.

Churchill was famous for his impassioned speeches, which rallied the British people. On June 18, 1940, he warned of the difficult struggle ahead: "Let us brace ourselves to our duties, and so bear ourselves, that if the British Empire and its Commonwealth last for a thousand years, men will still say, 'this was their finest hour.'"

ADOLF HITLER 1889–1945

Adolf Hitler (1889-1945) led Germany from 1933 until 1945. He was head of a political group called the National Socialist German Workers' Party, better known as the Nazi Party. Hitler was a brutal dictator. He was also a brilliant politician and a riveting speechmaker.

Hitler was a World War I (1914-1918) veteran. Germany suffered through a crushing economic depression after the war. The terms of surrender, called the Treaty of Versailles, put many burdens on Germany. Jobs were scarce. Hitler said the country was treated unfairly. He often blamed communists, Roma (gypsies), and most of all, Jewish people for Germany's problems.

Hitler was Germany's *Führer* (leader), but he had much help from Nazis who shared his extreme views. Hermann Göring was a close advisor and head of the *Luftwaffe*, the German air force. Heinrich Himmler was the chief of the dreaded *Gestapo* and SS secret police forces.

After rebuilding Germany's economy and powerful armed forces, Hitler ordered the invasion of Poland in 1939, starting World War II. He also ordered the Holocaust, the mass murder of six million Jews, along with hundreds of thousands of Roma and other persecuted groups.

Hitler did not manage the war very well, never fully trusting his generals or advisors. As World War II came to an end in 1945, Hitler's dream of a Third Reich, a Nazi regime that would last 1,000 years, came crashing down. He committed suicide in the German capital of Berlin on April 30, 1945.

JOSEPH

STALIN
1879–
1953

Joseph Stalin (1879-1953) led the communist Soviet Union from 1922 until his death in 1953. Like Germany's Hitler, Stalin was a brutal dictator. Millions of Soviet citizens who opposed him were murdered or sent to forced-labor camps.

Born poor and scarred from smallpox, as a young man Stalin entered a seminary to become a priest. He was expelled in 1899. He soon joined the communist political revolution that swept across Russia in the 1910s. He organized strikes against the ruling Russian tsar, incited riots, and spread propaganda. He was imprisoned several times. He changed his real last name, Dzhugashvili, to Stalin, a Russian word that means "steel."

Stalin quickly rose to power following the Russian Revolution of 1917 and the creation of the Soviet Union in 1922. His ambition seemed limitless, and his methods were often brutal. His enemies were exiled or murdered. He rapidly industrialized the country and made the Red Army stronger, but at a terrible price to his own citizens.

BENITO MUSSOLINI

1883–1945

Benito Mussolini (1883-1945) led Italy from 1922 until 1943. He started the Fascist movement, which promised order and unity for the Italian people, plus military glory. Fascists, however, were opposed to democracies—elected governments—and the rights of individual citizens. Like Hitler and Stalin, Mussolini was a dictator.

Mussolini was pompous and arrogant. His dream was to create a powerful Italian state, a reborn Roman Empire. He called himself *Il Duce*, Italian for "the leader." His zealous supporters were called "black shirts" because of the dark uniforms they wore. The Fascists ruled through fear and intimidation.

Many Italians liked Mussolini's law-and-order society. He passed some social reforms and improved public works. But his foreign policy proved disastrous. After invading Ethiopia in 1935, he formed an alliance with Adolf Hitler's Germany and then declared war on the Allies in 1940.

In 1943, Mussolini lost power and was imprisoned. He was soon rescued in a daring German commando raid. He then led a Fascist government in German-controlled northern Italy. But in 1945, as the Allies advanced, Mussolini was captured by Italian forces and executed.

LEADERS OF JAPAN

Emperor Hirohito

1901– 1989

Emperor Hirohito (1901-1989) ruled Japan from 1926 until his death in 1989. As a boy, he studied at Japan's finest schools. He liked marine biology, and even wrote several books on the subject. But in 1926, following the death of his father, he became emperor of all Japan.

Some Japanese worshiped Hirohito as a god sent to Earth to lead the nation. But in reality, he was a young and inexperienced man when World War II started. He could not control his generals, who wished to expand the Japanese Empire in Asia.

Hideki Tojo

1884– 1948

General Hideki Tojo (1884-1948) was a veteran of the Imperial Japanese Army. During World War II, he was appointed prime minister, effectively making him the leader of Japan. He approved an extremely aggressive foreign policy, which made him very popular at first with the Japanese people. It was his decision to launch the December 7, 1941, surprise attack on the naval base at Pearl Harbor, Hawaii, in the hope of weakening America's military strength.

After Japan's bitter defeat in 1945, the beloved Hirohito was allowed to remain emperor of Japan. Hideki Tojo, however, was convicted of war crimes and executed in 1948.

LEADERS OF CHINA

Chiang Kai-shek

1887–1975

Chiang Kai-shek (1887-1975) led the Chinese Nationalist government during World War II. At that time, China was a splintered country. Many areas were controlled by local warlords or communist supporters.

Chiang was born in eastern China in 1887. His father died when Chiang was young, leaving the family impoverished. Chiang trained for the military in Japan. He returned to his homeland in 1911 and helped the uprising that overthrew the imperial Qing Dynasty. In 1928, he became head of the Republic of China.

Mao Zedong
1893–1976

Mao Zedong (1893-1976) was a communist leader. His family were peasants from Hunan Province. Mao studied communist philosophy, military strategy, and politics. He was also an author and poet. Mao fought to overthrow Chiang Kai-shek's government in order to start a new, unified Chinese state based on communist beliefs.

Starting in 1937, Japan occupied much of northern and central China. It was a brutal invasion and many innocent Chinese civilians were killed. Mao and Chiang were forced to work together to defeat the Japanese invaders. But shortly after the Japanese were defeated, civil war broke out again between the Nationalist government and the communists.

With the end of the Chinese Civil War in 1949, Mao proclaimed the founding of the People's Republic of China. Chiang Kai-shek and his followers fled to the island of Formosa (today's Taiwan) off the mainland coast.

Mao Zedong continued to lead the People's Republic of China until his death in 1976. He created a strong government that transformed Chinese society into a modern state, but millions of citizens died during his turbulent rule.

Chiang Kai-shek continued to lead the Republic of China from his island exile until his death in 1975.

AMERICAN GENERALS

Dwight D. Eisenhower
1890–1969

Dwight D. Eisenhower (1890-1969) was the supreme commander of Allied forces in Europe. He rose to the rank of five-star general of the United States Army. Diplomatic but tough, Eisenhower planned and oversaw the D-Day invasion of France in 1944, and the following push of Allied forces into France and Germany, which led to the defeat of Adolf Hitler and the Nazis.

Eisenhower was born in Denison, Texas. His nickname was "Ike." He graduated from the U.S. Military Academy at West Point in 1915.

After the war, Eisenhower was very popular with the American public. In 1953, he became the 34th president of the United States.

George S. Patton
1885–1945

George S. Patton (1885-1945) was one of the best-known, and controversial, U.S. Army generals of World War II. An aggressive, brilliant field commander, his nickname was "old blood and guts." He famously wore a polished helmet, riding pants, and a pair of pearl-handled revolvers. His speeches were often laced with profanities. He was blunt and outspoken, which sometimes got him into trouble with his superiors.

Patton graduated from West Point in 1909. He was a tank commander during World War I (1914-1918). In World War II, he achieved the rank of four-star general. He had great success in the North Africa campaign against German Field Marshal Erwin Rommel, and in the invasion of Sicily. He also led the Allied tank charge into occupied France. His aggressive command of the American Third Army pushed the Nazis back into Germany.

After the war, on December 9, 1945, Patton was severely injured in a road accident. He died a few weeks later.

Omar Bradley
1893– 1981

During World War II, Omar Bradley (1893-1981) was the senior United States Army field commander in North Africa and Europe. He commanded the Twelfth United States Army Group, which made up most of the American forces that liberated France and helped defeat Nazi Germany.

Bradley graduated from the U.S. Military Academy at West Point, New York, in 1915. He was popular with his troops. Because of his reputation, he was often referred to as "a soldier's general." He eventually rose to the rank of five-star general, and served as Chairman of the Joint Chiefs of Staff. In 1951, he published his memoir, *A Soldier's Story*.

Douglas MacArthur
1880– 1964

General MacArthur wades ashore at the Philippines.

D ouglas MacArthur (1880-1964) commanded U.S. ground forces in the Pacific theater, fighting against Japan. He grew up in a military family, and graduated from West Point in 1903 at the top of his class. He rose to the rank of five-star general, and was awarded the Medal of Honor.

In December 1941, Japan invaded the Philippines. Many U.S. troops were killed or captured. MacArthur escaped in March 1942, but famously declared, "… I shall return."

Together with U.S. Navy Admiral Chester Nimitz, General MacArthur developed a strategy that bypassed Japanese strongholds in the Pacific. Instead, the Americans "island hopped," seizing certain islands and then using superior air and sea power to choke off Japanese supplies.

The island-hopping strategy worked. On October 20, 1944, MacArthur waded ashore at the Philippines. He had returned. Ten months later, Japan surrendered. MacArthur oversaw the American occupation and reform of Japan for the next several years.

MacArthur later commanded U.S. forces in the Korean War from 1950-1951. He died in Washington, D.C., in 1964.

UNITED KINGDOM
GENERALS

Bernard Montgomery
1887–1976

Bernard Law Montgomery (1887-1976) commanded the British Eighth Army in North Africa from 1942-1943. His nickname was "Monty." Although he was criticized for being too cautious in his battle planning, he raised troop morale with his lively personality. He was often seen mingling with soldiers under his command, wearing his distinctive black beret.

Montgomery won the Battle of El Alamein, in Egypt in 1942. In 1943, he led his army in the invasion of Sicily, along with General George Patton's American troops. Montgomery and Patton had a rivalry that lasted throughout the war. They often showed their disdain for one another, but worked together to defeat the Germans, their common enemy.

During the 1944 invasion of Normandy, France, Montgomery took command of the Allied 21st Army Group. He later earned the title of field marshal, the highest rank in the British army.

Harold Alexander

1891–1969

Harold Alexander (1891-1969) was a field marshal in charge of British forces in the Mediterranean theater. He was born in London, England, to noble parents. After schooling, he was trained as an army officer, and served during World War I.

During World War II, in the spring of 1940, Alexander helped oversee the British evacuation of more than 300,000 troops at Dunkirk, France, saving them from almost certain death or capture by German forces.

In the summer of 1942, Alexander was assigned to command British forces in the Mediterranean. His chief field commander was Bernard Montgomery. Alexander's forces drove the German and Italian armies out of Egypt and across North Africa. The British and Americans later liberated the island of Sicily and southern Italy.

GERMAN GENERALS

ERWIN
ROMMEL
1891–
1944

HEINZ
GUDERIAN
1888–
1954

Famed German tank commander Erwin Rommel (1891-1944) helped defeat France in 1940. In 1941, his Afrika Korps defeated superior numbers of British forces. Even Allied commanders admired the "Desert Fox's" daring battlefield skills. After returning to Germany, there was friction between Field Marshal Rommel and Adolf Hitler. Rommel was forced to commit suicide on October 14, 1944.

General Heinz Guderian (1888-1954) was a tank commander who helped develop the German battlefield tactic of *blitzkrieg* (lightning warfare). Using combined attacks of infantry, tanks, and planes, Germany scored quick victories in the early years of World War II. Guderian was a successful field commander as well, especially during the invasions of Poland and France.

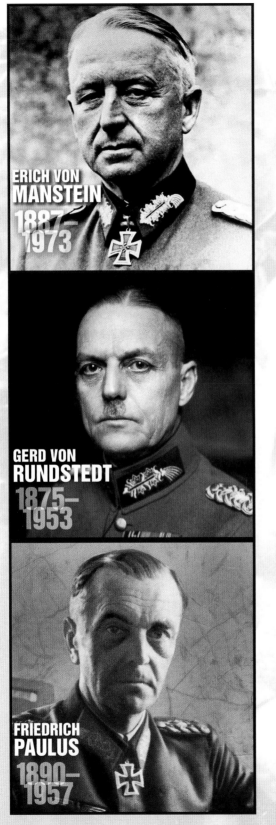

ERICH VON MANSTEIN 1887-1973

GERD VON RUNDSTEDT 1875-1953

FRIEDRICH PAULUS 1890-1957

Field Marshal Erich von Manstein (1887-1973) was one of Germany's most respected commanders. He was the chief planner of the invasion of Poland in 1939 and France in 1940. He often clashed with Hitler over strategy, and was dismissed in 1944.

Field Marshal Gerd von Rundstedt (1875-1953) was one of the most important planners of the German army. He commanded forces that invaded both Poland and the Soviet Union. He also planned the Atlantic coastal defenses of occupied France.

Field Marshal Friedrich Paulus (1890-1957) commanded the German Sixth Army during the Battle of Stalingrad. Facing bitter defeat, Hitler ordered Paulus to fight to the death. Paulus defied Hitler and surrendered what remained of his army to the Soviets on January 31, 1943.

SOVIET UNION
GENERALS

GEORGY ZHUKOV 1896–1974

ANDREY YERYOMENKO 1892–1970

Georgy Zhukov (1896-1974) was Marshal of the Soviet Union during World War II, the highest rank in the Red Army. Zhukov masterminded many of the Soviet Union's military victories, pushing the invading Germans all the way back to their capital of Berlin. Zhukov often stood up to Soviet dictator Joseph Stalin to keep him from interfering in war plans.

General Andrey Yeryomenko (1892-1970) held several commands in the Red Army during World War II, but he is most famous for his defense of the city of Stalingrad in 1942-1943. Yeryomenko was wounded several times during the war. Once, he refused to go to a hospital until after the battle finished. After the war, he achieved the rank of Marshal of the Soviet Union.

VASILY CHUIKOV 1900–1982

CONSTANTINE ROKOSSOVSKY 1896–1968

General Vasily Chuikov (1900-1982) commanded the Soviet 62nd Army during the Battle of Stalingrad in 1942-1943. Sometimes described as a "rough-edged" commander, he urged his troops to fight the Germans street-to-street, and house-to-house. By "hugging the enemy," Chuikov stripped the Germans of their "lightning warfare" superiority. After the war, Chuikov was awarded the rank of Marshal of the Soviet Union.

General Constantine Rokossovsky (1896-1968) commanded the Soviet Central Front at the Battle of Kursk in 1943, the largest tank battle of the war and a major victory for the Soviet Union. He also planned and led several other critical battles. For his brilliant battlefield strategies, Rokossovsky was awarded the rank of Marshal of the Soviet Union in 1944.

GLOSSARY

ALLIES

The Allies were the many nations that were allied, or joined, in the fight against Germany, Italy, and Japan in World War II. The most powerful nations among the Allies included the United States, the United Kingdom, the Soviet Union, France, China, Canada, and Australia.

AXIS

The Axis powers were the World War II alliance of Germany, Italy, and Japan.

BLITZKRIEG

A German word meaning "lightning warfare." It described a new strategy that the German military used in World War II. *Blitzkrieg* called for very large invasions to overwhelm the enemy quickly with combined land and air attacks in order to avoid long, drawn-out battles.

COMMUNISM

The Soviet Union was ruled by members of a political party called the Communist Party. Communism is a form of socialism that seeks to abolish classes in society, and to get rid of private ownership such as land or businesses. All individuals are supposed to be equal, and everyone shares in the work according to their abilities. The government has total control over the economy, and restricts personal freedoms.

D-DAY

A day when a military operation begins. Most people today associate D-Day with the Normandy, France, invasion of June 6, 1944.

Fascist

Italian dictator Benito Mussolini's political party was called the Fascist Party. Over the years, the term "fascist" has become a general term that means anyone who supports a dictatorship and attacking enemies with forceful military action.

Great Depression

The Great Depression was a period of severe economic downturn, starting in 1929 and lasting about a decade. During the Great Depression, jobs were scarce, manufacturing plants were closed, and few people had extra money.

Nazi

The Nazi Party was the political party in Germany that supported Adolf Hitler. After 1934 it was the only political party allowed in Germany. This is when Hitler became a dictator and ruled Germany with total power.

SS

A Nazi secret police organization that was originally created to be Adolf Hitler's bodyguard. The initials SS stand for the German word *schutzstaffen*, which means "protection squad." As the war progressed, the SS was placed in charge of concentration camps and the extermination of Jewish people and other persecuted groups.

Third Reich

A term that refers to Germany during the years the Nazi Party and Adolf Hitler were in power, from 1933 to 1945. *Reich* is a German word meaning "empire." Many Germans believed that the country had two other periods in its history in which it controlled a powerful empire, once in medieval times and once in the period leading up to World War I. The Third Reich implied that Nazi Germany was the next step in Germany's power and glory.

INDEX